Microcosm Publishing is Portland's most diversified publishing house and distributor with a focus on the colorful, authentic, and empowering. Our books and zines have put your power in your hands since 1996, equipping readers to make positive changes in their lives and in the world around them. Microcosm emphasizes skill-building, showing hidden histories, and fostering creativity through challenging conventional publishing wisdom with books and bookettes about DIY skills, food, bicycling, gender, self-care, and social justice. What was once a distro and record label was started by Joe Biel in his bedroom and has become among the oldest independent publishing houses in Portland, OR. We are a politically moderate, centrist publisher in a world that has inched to the right for the past 80 years.

Introduction

What would you bring with you to a desert island? What books, music, movies, or objects would make the cut? This is one of those game-like hypothetical questions that for some people in history have been all too real—and it turns out that when you find yourself actually stranded on a desert island, not having a wide selection of media is the least of your worries.

The five true stories in this zine are about teenagers who survived shipwrecks far from home, and spent the next year or more... in some cases, much more... living in the strange new world they found themselves capsized into.

Each of these teens needed to be resourceful and resilient, both in the immediate aftermath of the wreck and in the longer term adjustment afterwards—in many cases, to a whole new language, culture, and family—and then back again, for the ones who returned. None of these teens were stranded alone like Tom Hanks in the movie *Cast Away*, and many of the new things they had to learn were not just about finding food and building shelter, but fitting in with a new social group. And matters of basic survival were compounded by grief. None of them had any way of knowing what was happening back at the home they had left behind, and had no way of learning, sometimes for years or decades, if their families and friends were alive or dead. And they must have imagined their home communities thinking they had died and holding funerals for them.

I wrote this zine while researching a longer book called *Dropouts & Runaways*, which is about teens who left their homes or schools or both (whether or not they wanted to) and made new lives for themselves. One of the many themes that came out of these stories was teens who started their independent lives at a young age because of an accident—a shipwreck—and not because of conflict, cruelty, or necessity. (Though if you read between the lines, you can make some guesses about which of the teens in this zine had a stable, loving home to start out with.) These stories may not all end up in the final book, but they are too amazing not to share.

Manjirō

Manjirō's adventure began in January, 1841, when five men set out together to fish in the deep ocean. Three were brothers: Fudenojo was 37, Jusuke was 24, and another teen, 15-year-old Goemon. Toraemon, 25, was their neighbor. And Manjirō, at 14, was tagging along from a nearby village, learning their trade. They had borrowed a 24-foot boat, loaded it with enough water, rice, and firewood to last them for several days, and pushed off the southeast coast of the Japanese island of Shikoku.

Because of the two inexperienced teens on board, they went slowly. The trip started out successful, and they were catching fish about 18 miles from land when the wind picked up and they were caught in a sudden storm, damaging their boat so they could not navigate and tossing them out to sea. They drifted for over a week, their food and water quickly disappearing.

And then they sighted land, a green volcanic cone rising out of the ocean. They barely made it to shore; they had to tie together their broken oar to bring them in, and when they jumped out of the boat to swim the rest of the way, it capsized and broke Jusuke's leg. He nearly passed out from the pain, but Fudenojo helped him make the swim.

The island they found themselves on is now called Tori Shima, which means bird island; it's about 375 miles off the coast of Japan. True to its name, they found not much but grass, sand, and thousands of birds—the now-endangered short-tailed albatross. Discovering a cave, they crawled into it, ate some birds raw, and slept.

The next day they set about figuring out how to survive. They built a shelter from driftwood and began to perfect the art of hunting birds, which they cooked by pounding the meat into a paste and spreading it on a rock in the sun. They called it "stone roast."

In their more than 100 days on the island, it rained on only 30 or 40 of those days; to survive the rest, they drank their own urine. Exploring, they found the graves of prior inhabitants, castaways like themselves. They survived a massive earthquake that nearly trapped them in their cave. Several times they sighted ships in the distance that did not see or stop for them. After the birds migrated away from the island, they grazed on seaweed and shellfish. They began to despair.

On June 27th, Captain William H. Whitfield of the US American whaling ship *John Howland* out of Fairhaven, Mass recorded in his log,

> "This day light wind from SE. The isle in sight. At 1pm sent in 2 boats to see if there was any turtle, found 5 poor distressed people on the isle, took them off, could not understand anything from them more than that they were hungry."

Jusuke's leg hadn't healed well, and Fudenojo was too weak to walk. The three others mustered the strength to swim out to the ship, and after an elaborate pantomimed conversation, the sailors helped them retrieve their two companions from the cave. Inside the ship, the castaways found the multiracial crew, wearing bizarre clothes and speaking unintelligibly, to be fearsomely beyond their understanding. The captain's richly appointed quarters seemed like a shrine. They were given dry clothes, but they had to be shown how to put them on—they had only ever worn kimonos before.

When they were served broth—the only thing they had a chance of digesting after being so near starvation—the castaways began to realize that they would not be immediately killed by these strange sailors. But the next day, a boat was readied, and the captain gestured to Manjirō to get aboard to return to the island. Manjirō wept, until the captain pantomimed that he was to go fetch the clothes and other possessions the castaways had left behind.

For the next six months, the *John Howland* was their home; they traveled near Japan but could not legally or safely bring their passengers there no matter how much they longed to go home.

Had Manjirō and his friends been shipwrecked at a different moment in history, the captain would likely have brought them back to Japan, or at least to ships nearby. But for the past 200 years, Japanese law had prohibited exactly that.

> "No Japanese ship...nor any native of Japan, shall presume to go out of the country; whoever acts contrary to this, shall die, and the ship with the crew and goods aboard shall be sequestered until further orders. All persons who return from abroad shall be put to death."

So read Japan's Seclusion Act of 1636, launching the policy of sakoku, which translates to "closed country." In the early 1600s, Japan had been very open, part of a global network of trade and cultural exchange, but also mired in civil war and piracy. The powerful Tokugawa shogunate—the feudal military family that ran the government—wanted to consolidate power and wealth. They had been watching what was happening in the Americas: Spanish and Portuguese colonization was rampant, and it went hand in hand with religious conversions, enslavement, disease, and the annexation of land and natural resources. The final straw was the Shimabara Rebellion, an uprising of 40,000 mostly Catholic peasants protesting high taxes and religious restrictions. The shogunate cracked down. Catholicism was made illegal, and Japanese converts who would not renounce it were executed. The only trade allowed was with the Netherlands, China, Korea, the Indigenous Ainu in the north, and the Ryukyu Islands in the south, and only through a few specific ports, controlled by the Tokugawas. Foreigners could not visit or live in Japan, and Japanese people were not permitted to leave the country.

This prohibition posed a particular problem for castaways and shipwrecked sailors—like Manjirō. If their own ship were destroyed, no foreign ship could legally carry them home. And if they did make it back to their own country, as some managed to, they found themselves with new difficulties.

So the *John Howland* went about its business without straying into Japanese waters. It was a whaling ship out of New Bedford, Massachusetts. It was 111 feet long, held 6,000 barrels, livestock, grain, 2 cannons, and 30 bayonets, with a crew of 34 men. Whale oil was a primary source of fuel at that time, burned for lanterns, cooking fuel, and heating. As the ship continued its travels, the crew caught and processed 15 or 16 whales, filling thousands of those barrels with oil. The castaways watched, learned, began to pick up some English, and recovered from their near brush with starvation.

In November, the ship made port in Oahu, in what is now the US state of Hawai'i. Captain Whitfield introduced the castaways to a friend in the local government, who welcomed them warmly and found them a house. Whitfield commissioned them each a suit of clothes as a parting gift and gave them each a bit of money.

Whitfield was impressed with Manjirō's intelligence and spirit, and they got along well. Before he left Oahu, he invited him to return to the US with him, see more of the world, and go to school. Manjirō seized the opportunity and, with Fudenojo's reluctant permission, signed on as a member of the ship's crew.

The crew, now counting Manjirō in its numbers, left Oahu in December, 1841 to sail west again in search of whales. Poignantly, the ship went within sight of the island where the five had been stranded, and Manjirō's home in Japan must have felt painfully near, yet completely inaccessible. But he was also fitting in with the crew, speaking English more fluently and learning their work. They had trouble with his name, so they shortened it to the first syllable, spelling it "Mung;" Manjirō would use the name John Mung for much of the next decade. After killing several more whales, they headed towards the US. They passed the southern tip of South America in April, 1842 and arrived in Massachusetts in June with 2,761 barrels of sperm whale oil. The *John Howland* had been away for 3 and a half years. Manjirō was now 16.

Fairhaven, Massachusetts, was another world from what Manjirō was used to. He lived in Whitfield's home with the Captain and his wife Albertina. As was fairly typical at the time, he worked part-time while attending the local school. He continued to improve his English, learned reading, writing, arithmetic, navigation, and surveying, practiced farming and animal husbandry, and trained in cooperage (making watertight barrels)—an education designed to support a career in whaling. It is probable that he also went to church and regularly visited his neighbors. In his story of his ten years away, he does not go into great detail about his time here. We do know that his school got a very poor report from the district around the time he was there. The inspector did not like that the teachers were all whalers, and that the building was "old, and out of repair. … There is a black-board, but it has been used the last winter but very little, if any."

Whitfield left again in 1844 on another 4 year whaling journey, leaving Manjirō behind; but two years later, a friend from the *John Howland* who now captained his own whaler, the *Franklin*, came to see Manjirō. At 19, he was an adult now, and ready to see more of the world and put his education into practice. He signed up to be the ship's steward, in exchange for a 1/140th share of the voyage's profits. They set out in October of 1846, sailing this time around the coast of Africa and back into the Pacific. Once again, he passed through waters close to Japan and his ship even stopped to fish off the shore of Tori Shima.

Eventually, the *Franklin* stopped in Oahu for 20 days, and Manjirō was reunited with Toraemon. They caught up on everything that had happened to each of them in the five years since they'd parted ways.

The four castaways who remained in Oahu had at first fished and done farm work while they learned English, and eventually all had found steady jobs. Jusuke had died in 1845. The injury to his leg from jumping out of the boat when they wrecked at Tori Shima had never healed properly, and he finally succumbed to the wound. This was a hard time for the others, mourning their friend and brother. But later that year, Captain Whitfield had come back through the port, bringing news of Manjirō, gifts of money, clothes, and tobacco, and a happy surprise: He had arranged passage for them on a ship back to Japan.

Toraemon had developed a stable career as a carpenter and was deeply skeptical about being able to return, and he elected to stay behind. But Fudenojo (who had changed his name to the more locally-pronounceable

Denzo) and Goemon were overjoyed. They had never stopped longing to return to Japan. In Oahu, they had met other Japanese castaways who had inspired them to keep trying. They gave away their land and house, quickly said their goodbyes, and set off on the whaling ship *Florida*. But their trip was in vain; they sighted land several times in various parts of Japan, but could not land at any port due to either weather or threats from local authorities.

When Denzo and Goemon returned to Oahu, bummed from their failed voyage, they found Manjirō still in port. They all celebrated and cried together, mourning their lost friend and their lost home. Manjirō had to sail out again, but they all agreed they would meet again in Japan.

The *Franklin* left again and the hunt for whales continued. In a dramatic turn of events, the ship's captain had a mental breakdown and the crew chained him up until they could leave him at the American consulate in Guam. The first mate became the captain and the hunt continued. Going back around the horn of Africa, they returned to Massachusetts in June, 1849. They had killed 500 whales, and Manjirō had earned 350 dollars. It was a lot of money—almost $12,000 in today's money— but not quite enough, he thought, to realize his dream of somehow buying passage home to Japan.

But on his recent voyage, he had learned of a way that he might earn more: The Gold Rush. Like so many others, the promise of a land covered in precious ore inspired him to try his luck. In late 1849, he and a friend found work on a ship going around South America to California. In San Francisco, they got on a steamship to Sacramento; from there they rode on horseback and then hiked out to the Sierra Nevada. They didn't like the brothels or the generally violent and lawless atmosphere of the frontier town, but the money was very, very good. After working as miners for an agency for 30 days, they had earned $180 in wages. They'd heard they could do better working independently, so they struck out on their own. This was a good strategy: Manjirō earned more than $600 in 70 days, which his biographer described later as "an enormous sum of money. He thought it would be indecent to continue." It would have been over $20,000 today. He had, in any event, achieved his goal, earning enough to buy passage back to Japan for himself and his three surviving fellow castaways, if he could find a ship to take them. He had traveled around the world twice, but now for the first time, he paid a fare for an ocean voyage—as a passenger on a whaling ship from San Francisco to Oahu, an 18-day journey that cost him $25 (about $850 today).

It was now 1850. Arriving again in Oahu to pick up his friends, he found Toraemon first, who took him to the town where Denzo and Goemon had moved. Again, Toraemon was pessimistic; he didn't see any point in trying to go home. Reluctantly, the rest proceeded with Manjirō's plan without him.

It wasn't easy, as you couldn't just buy a ticket to Japan. The three friends started looking for a ship that would be willing to divert its course into Japanese waters in exchange for a hefty fee. Manjirō spent $125 (today, it would be $4,200) of his savings on a small boat that they could bring on the ship and use to get the rest of the way to shore. Providentially, a large US American ship came to port the next month whose crew included a number of other Japanese sailors. Before the shipwreck that had stranded them, they had met another castaway who had successfully returned to Japan and inherited his uncle's estate. This gave the friends even more hope.

Denzo and Goemon must not have really believed they would make it this time, because they did not say goodbye to their friends and family; Goemon had married, and he told his wife that they were shipping out for a long voyage but that he expected to return. But Manjirō was optimistic. He left behind his money, his western clothes, and his books and papers for Captain Whitfield to distribute upon his next visit to Oahu, along with a letter saying "I never forgot your benevolence of bringing me up from a small boy to manhood. I have done nothing for your kindness until now. Now I am going to return with Denzo and Goemon to my country. ... I believe good will come out of this changing world, and that we will meet again."

In January, 1851 their ship drew up within 7 miles of one of the Ryukyu Islands—what is now Okinawa province in the south of Japan, but was then an independent nation. They likely chose it because it was one of the few countries to have trade agreements with Japan, as well as being very nearby. As they sighted land, Manjirō hastily scribbled a note to be brought back to Toraemon, explaining the ease of the journey and urging him to follow soon. Then they let their small boat over the side, with the US ship waiting at anchor to make sure they made it safely to land.

But the sea was rough and Denzo and Goemon freaked out, no doubt vividly remembering their last trip all together in a small boat in rough waters. Manjirō, used to life at sea, kept a cool head and took over, navigating them the remaining miles safely to land.

Exhausted, they landed on the sandy beach of a cove. People came to find them right away, but were at first afraid of their strange clothes, appearance, and speech. Finally someone was found who spoke Japanese. Fear quickly turned to excitement as locals competed to offer food and hospitality to these adventurous and bold strangers. But soon government officials were alerted and the three were taken into custody and escorted to the regional office, a seven mile hike away. It was the middle of the night, they were exhausted, and the road was muddy. On arrival, they were interrogated until dawn. After this, they were treated relatively well, kept under guard in a farmer's house and given good meals, Japanese clothes, alcohol, and mosquito nets. Eventually, a boat was found that could take them on the final leg of their trip: the 3-week voyage to Japan.

In Japan, they were still prisoners, but treated as distinguished guests. And there were some high points. They were under suspicion for potentially bringing in illegal religious or seditious influences, but they were also exciting for this same reason—everyone wanted to hear their stories. And some of the fellow Japanese castaways they had befriended on Oahu had also made it home, through China, and they could celebrate together. Their interrogation continued for a year. They had to give very detailed accounts of everywhere they had been and all they had done. They were required to step on a plaque bearing Christian imagery to prove they had not converted. At last, a tribunal decided that they would be allowed to return to their home province. They were forbidden to leave the country again or have any occupation related to the sea; but they were given a lifetime stipend and permission to go to their home villages.

This was the final leg of their long, long voyage home from a fishing expedition gone awry. Manjirō had spent that decade wondering if his mother and siblings were all still alive. They were, and the reunion of all the returned castaways with their relatives and friends was tearful and joyous.

Manjirō was now 25 years old. He had spent ten years abroad, fully six of them at sea, and over a year imprisoned in Japan.

We don't know if Toraemon ever made it back to Japan (or if he actually wanted to). Denzo and Goemon lived out their days quietly in their home village. But Manjirō's star was on the rise. Only three days after his return home, he was summoned by the lord of his province to come to the capitol and teach English and foreign affairs to young samurai leaders. In exchange, he was made a low-ranking samurai. This was a rare thing in feudal Japan, with its strict class structure, for the hereditary position of samurai to be given to a child of a poor fishing village.

History was continuing to move, as well. Just as Manjirō was beginning to teach, a U.S. American captain, Matthew Perry, was leaving Virginia with four huge, steam-powered, black-painted battleships on a mission to re-open Japan to US trade by any means. The Black Ships arrived the next year at Edo, which is now Tokyo—a city where foreign traders were forbidden. Steam power was unknown in Japan and the sight of the four massive ships hurtling at full speed, under their own power, was intimidating enough; Captain Perry's threats, conveyed via multiple layers of translation, to burn Edo to the ground were also compelling. He was eventually allowed to land and deliver a demand letter. One year later he returned with eight steamships to make good on that letter's ultimatum. Negotiations began; within a month, Japan had signed a trade agreement with the US, and over the next few years began to trade again with more and more countries.

During these early negotiations, Manjirō was summoned to meet with government leaders and to tell them everything he had learned in his teens about US politics, history, and culture. He obliged, and took a major personal risk by adding his opinion that Japan's isolationist policies should end. The officials were impressed. He was invited to speak at greater length, and given a promotion and a family name: Nakahama, the name of his native village. He was also enlisted to use his knowledge of western technology to help build up the military fortifications along Japan's coast. He translated the US American book on technical navigation, wrote the first English language textbook published in Japan, and was appointed a professor at Japan's Naval Training School, where he taught popular classes on navigation and English. His students and readers were some of the most effective promoters of modernization and democracy in Japan.

His influence was massive, but his life was politically complicated. He was always regarded with suspicion by conservative nationalists, and had to keep a bodyguard to protect against assassination.

So he may have been happy to have the chance to travel again in 1860, joining one of the first two diplomatic missions from Japan to the US as an interpreter. It was the first trip an all-Japanese crew had taken on the open sea in over two centuries, and the crew was seasick and generally lacking in experience. When a storm came, it was Manjirō and the few foreign sailors aboard who stepped up and saved the ship.

In 1870, he was sent as a government observer to Europe to monitor the war between France and Prussia. On the way, his ship stopped in New York and he took a train to Fairhaven to visit Captain Whitfield. Manjirō was now 43 and Whitfield was 65. It was a happy reunion, and he got to stay one more night in his childhood room.

But his career was cut short. The year after his trip to Europe, Manjirō suffered a small stroke and retired from public life. He lived quietly in Tokyo until his death in 1898 at age 71. He had been married 3 times and had 7 children.

Manjirō's celebrity had been fleeting. When he first returned to Japan, he was the best educated source on western ways. But soon more Japanese citizens traveled abroad and learned even more than he had been able to. Influential as he was, Manjirō soon outlived his political usefulness, and he didn't have the class background or political savvy to carve out a lasting position of influence. He had a vision of bringing democracy to Japan, and had he lived into the 20th century, it's likely he would not have approved of the extremely aggressive military direction his country took, particularly relying on the modern navy he had helped build. Poignantly, his grave was destroyed by US air raids in 1943, during World War II.

"He was like a revolutionary who could not participate in a revolution," wrote his grandson in a 1970 biography. Still, he is remembered and revered for his role, and there are statues of him in Japan and Massachusetts. Every year to this day, the Japan-America Grassroots Summit meets alternately between the two countries to commemorate the friendship between Manjirō and Captain Whitfield.

Otokichi

Manjirō was far from the only Japanese castaway who was able to return home in these two hundred years of isolation. Despite the harsh wording of the isolation law, there don't seem to be any documented instances of shipwrecked sailors being executed upon return; it was understood that it wasn't their choice, though they were all under suspicion for bringing western agendas back with them. Manjirō had a wealthy benefactor in his friend Captain Whitfield, who gave him educational and economic opportunities that most other shipwreck survivors did not have. But still, many shipwreck survivors had similar experiences of being rescued by ships out of the US or South America, and continuing to work on ships and save and scheme to be able to return to Japan.

As a young person, Otokichi worked as an apprentice cook on a ship transporting rice from one part of Japan to another. In 1832, when he was 14, his ship was blown out to sea in a storm and the mast was broken. The crew drifted for nearly 5,000 miles over the course of 14 months, surviving on their cargo of rice and seawater distilled in a sake maker. They suffered from scurvy, and only three of the original fourteen crew members, two of them teenagers, were still alive when they ran aground on the Olympic peninsula in what is now The US state of Washington.

The three castaways—Iwakichi, Kyukichi, and Otokichi (they went down in history as the "three Kichis")—were found on the beach by people from the Indigenous Makah community. Their rescuers salvaged what they could find on the ship, fed and nursed the castaways back to health, and put them to work gathering berries and other domestic tasks. After a few months, the Makah traded the shipwreck's survivors to the settler colonial government at Fort Vancouver. The British settlers believed that they had rescued them from slavery, but it's unclear if the castaways had more actual freedom with the British than with the Makah.

At Fort Vancouver, the castaways were indoctrinated into Christianity. Eventually they learned enough English to communicate that they were from Japan, not China, as the settlers had assumed. Originally, the English offered to find them a ship home, but being nationals of a closed country made them seem more politically valuable. The chief agent at Fort Vancouver, John McLoughlin, hoped they would be useful, perhaps as informants or hostages, in reopening trade with his own home country, England. So instead of being returned home, they were sent instead around the tip of South America to England.

But in 1835, the British authorities were deeply caught up in conflict with China over the opium trade, and they were not at all interested in Japan. They shipped the three directly on to the Portuguese colony of Macau, on the Chinese coast, sending a bill for their keep and travel back to McLoughlin. The three Kichis had now very nearly circumnavigated the globe, through no agency or will of their own. From Macau, they made an attempt to return to Japan, but the ship carrying them was rebuffed with cannonballs from the two ports it approached.

Not being welcome at home was a huge disappointment, but Otokichi was sharp and resilient. He found steady work on ships, started a trading business, and became a well-regarded translator. He settled down in Shanghai, married a German-Malay woman named Louisa Belder, raised four children, translated part of the Bible into Japanese, and changed his name to John Matthew Ottoson.

Though he did not try to return to Japan again himself, he used his connections and resources to help other Japanese castaways successfully return home through China. His career did bring him back to Japan again twice more, though. The first time, he snuck in pretending to be a Chinese interpreter on a survey ship in 1849. He returned again in 1854, under his new British name, as a translator in the negotiation of the first treaty between Japan and Britain, shortly after the treaty was signed between Japan and the US.

On this second visit, he was offered the opportunity to return to live permanently in Japan. But by now, his entire adult life was elsewhere, and he declined. If he had converted to Christianity, it would have been too dangerous to return; in any event he probably felt betrayed and rejected by his home country.

He was also offered British citizenship, which he accepted. Along with the large fee he received for negotiating the treaty, this enabled him to retire to a big colonial house in Singapore with his family. He died there of tuberculosis at age 49, in 1867.

In 1983, a big-budget Hollywood movie about the three Kichis was made, called *Kairei* and starring Johnny Cash as McLoughlin. It flopped. Otokichi's life, however, was a success. Despite the bad luck and trauma of his time at sea, and being captured and used by the authorities he encountered during the following year, he was savvy enough to make use of his rare combination of languages, as well as his skills at seafaring and in business, and created a new international life, family, and career on his own terms.

Narcisse Pelletier / Anco

Narcisse Pelletier was barely 14 in 1858 when his life changed dramatically. He had grown up the oldest of four brothers in the small town of Saint-Gilles on the coast of France. His father was a shoemaker, but his uncle was harbor master and would take him out on the boat he'd named after him: *Le jeune Narcisse*. He was a sensitive child with an aptitude for sailing, and it was assumed from a young age that he would embark on a career at sea.

This was his second job as a cabin boy on a long haul voyage, and it was already going disastrously. Several months before, the first mate on his ship attacked him and "gave him a nasty stab wound," as Narcisse put it later. Injured and traumatized, he'd transferred ships at the next port. At first, things on his new ship went as smoothly as it could for someone recovering from a knife wound while working on his feet all day. They dropped off their cargo of wine in Bombay, then went to Hong Kong to recruit Chinese workers to bring to the gold mines in Australia.

This is where things started to go really haywire, perhaps predictably so. The captain had brought on far more passengers than the boat could safely hold—over 300, "piled on top of each other" as Narcisse described it later—and not nearly enough food for everyone. When the boat was becalmed at sea, the passengers were put on half rations and threatened mutiny. So the captain decided to shorten the trip by taking a dangerous shortcut through the Solomon Islands rather than going around by the open sea.

But the sea was no longer calm. Big waves and thick fog enveloped the ship for three days. At 1am, Narcisse and the first mate were on watch. A large, dark shape loomed on the horizon; they assumed it was a storm. By the time they realized it was actually a cliff they were sailing straight into, it was too late. The ship struck the rock and began to break apart.

Everyone on board had to evacuate to the nearest island, bringing as much food as they could salvage. The island was tiny and waterless. When Narcisse and a few others were sent to find water on a larger island nearby, they were attacked by the people who lived there. Several of his shipmates were killed, and Narcisse was struck in the head by a rock. He and another boy survived by running into the ocean, even though they could not swim. Their captain picked them up as the rest of the crew used guns to fend off a more organized attack on the shipwreck's survivors.

The captain, in his report much later, said that he had consulted with his Chinese passengers and developed a plan to take a small party and seek help for the whole group at an English settlement. But as Narcisse told the story, that small group left stealthily in the dead of night; he only joined them because he happened to wake up just in time and jump on board, panicked at nearly being left behind.

The 11 men in the boat left their provisions and guns behind. They must have planned or hoped to find help nearby. But they were in that tiny boat for 12 days, surviving on raw sea birds and drinking their own urine, covering 600 miles until they reached what is now called Cape York, at the very northeastern tip of the Australian continent. They'd long run out of food and water, and they hopped along the coast finding little of either. When they searched on land, Narcisse couldn't keep up. He was exhausted, starving, dehydrated, still reeling from his concussion, and with injured feet from walking on coral. His shipmates clearly thought he wouldn't survive. At one watering hole they came to, they drank it dry before he caught up with them, and told him to wait for it to refill while they explored onward. Then they went back to their ship and sailed on without him. Eventually they would find help, though it was too late for the Chinese passengers they'd left behind, who all died. And it was too late for Narcisse.

He woke from his nap by the watering hole to find himself suddenly alone, and the raw horror of this stayed with him for his entire life. Desperately praying, he staggered off inland into the forest, his already-injured feet sliced open again by thorns that lay on the ground. After spending the night in the rain, he kept walking, he did not know where to.

But he found people—three women, who ran from him. Some time later, two middle-aged men with spears cautiously approached him. Narcisse could not speak or understand their language, but he was desperate to connect. He offered them his only possessions: a tin cup and a handkerchief. Charmed, they gave him water and food, but they feared that he was bait in a European trap, and took him farther from the shore for the night. They built a large fire to ward off mosquitos, and at last Narcisse slept, feeling almost safe.

But that feeling ended abruptly when he woke the next morning and found himself all alone again. Weeping, he ran on bleeding feet all the way back to the shore, where he found his rescuers. Seeing him, they ran towards him with excited greetings, and he was relieved—they had been out gathering breakfast to share with him.

His rescuers were a family traveling together, two men and three women all related by marriage. They were part of the Wanthaala clan of the Pama Malngkaga, or Sandbeach People. One of the men, Maademan, adopted Narcisse as his own child that day on the beach, and gave him a new name, Anco. In their culture, shared family connection is what made someone truly human and relatable. So at the time, when encountering outsiders, adopting them into their family structure was the only way to create a meaningful relationship.

Anco must not have understood any of this until much later, but he knew that he was being accepted and cared for, a sudden change from the violence and alienation of his recent life. He led his rescuers back to the dry spring where he had been abandoned and gave them the blankets that had been left behind there. He had now offered them everything he had to give, except his clothes. His new family showed him their appreciation for this new gift in words he couldn't understand and gestures that were easier to grasp. His biographer wrote, "On seeing these declarations of affection, whose sincerity he could no longer doubt, all fear was banished from his heart."

Anco was still too weak to travel, so the three sisters-in-law stayed with him so he could rest for two days while Maademan and his brother-in-law went back home to tell people the news of adopting the lost, white child. After two days of rest, he was strong enough to travel to meet the rest of the Wanthaala—there were about 30 of them at any given time. When he arrived there, people were fascinated and didn't know what to make of him, but welcomed him with good humor. His biographer wrote of the women who greeted him, "At the sight of his young and beardless face they were convinced that the person they had before them was one of their own sex and two of them, who for a moment found themselves alone with the new arrival, wanted to make certain of this. On seeing their mistake, they burst into laughter and took themselves off very quickly."

He learned so much, later on; this funny episode was key to understanding his role in this society where your gender was as important as who you were related to in determining who you could and couldn't talk with, joke with, and what you could eat. He also learned much later that another white man had lived with the Wanthaala a generation before. So his presence there, while rare and strange, wasn't unprecedented. In the Pama Malngkana religion, white people were seen as likely to be dead family members come back to life, and this may have contributed to their immediate, warm acceptance of him.

It took him a long time to recover from his shock and injuries, to get used to eating solid food at all, much less an unfamiliar diet. But eventually he healed. He learned the language, and he absorbed his new culture like a sponge. He kept some of his European habits for a long time—he was teased incessantly for the way he bathed and washed his hands. One day while he was bathing, some people stole his clothes, now quite ragged, and tore them up to make headbands, and then he fit in even better.

Over the years that followed, Anco grew up to be a Pama Malngkana man. The soles of his feet grew tough enough to run barefoot over thorns without pain. His ear and septum were pierced, and he was given horizontal scarification marks on his belly, chest, and upper arms, created by slicing the skin with a sharp shell and pinching the wounds in front of a fire. He received the same religious initiation as all the young men of his family, though he could never fully complete the process, which began with birth—for instance, he never had one of his upper front teeth removed, and stood out because of it.

He made a close friend his own age, his cousin Chachil. Together they fished, repaired canoes, made spears, and did the other work of daily life. Chachil saved his life once, intervening in a fight where Anco had been attacked for taking food that wasn't his share. The rules around how food was divided, and who could and couldn't eat various types of food depending on age, gender, and social connection, were complex and took him a long time to master. As punishment for a similar crime, a cut on his leg became infected. He learned that this was because of malicious witchcraft—this is how all illness, injury, and premature death was understood.

He was proud of his great physical strength, his scarifications, the growing length of the piercing in his ear, and the skill he developed at making spearheads—this was his real expertise—but he never could swim as well as his peers.

Maademan arranged for him to marry, but as he tried to explain to his biographer, it didn't look anything like a marriage in 19th century France; it was more like a long engagement or political alliance. Marriages were, at least for their first decade, entirely chaste—they were arranged between grown men and girls of 2 or 3 years old. The primary goal of marriage was to form a strong bond between the girl's father and the husband, and between their respective clans, and it was considered unbreakable. Though the man and the toddler could get to know each other for a few years, after the girl was around seven they were forbidden from interacting until she came of age. Anco's marriage didn't have this chance. It may not have been a happy union anyway—he reported to his biographer that his young wife didn't like him; he was too different. But he wasn't celibate, either—he told other sources that he had fathered two or three children.

This was his life for seventeen years. He may have always been a bit of an oddball outsider, different-looking and sometimes picked on, but he had good friends and he worked hard to fit in, fully embracing his new life, home, religion, and family. According to his biographer, "Although recollections of his country of birth were not entirely wiped from his memory, the days of his childhood appeared to him to belong to such a distant past that he was sometimes inclined to wonder if Saint-Gilles really did exist, if its church, its harbour and its ships were not just a figment of his imagination."

In seventeen years, he only once saw white men on land. He wanted to talk to them, but Maademan wouldn't allow it. This was a time of increased contact between European settlers and Indigenous Australians, a connection that would later be devastating to the Pama Malngkana, though remote as they were they were isolated from some of the worst effects of colonialism, like kidnapping of children into residential schools. There were far fewer contacts being made in Anco's time, and they weren't all benign—he told his first adult European friend that his clan was afraid "not of white men, but of white men's guns." But there was some trading, for candy, tobacco, and cloth.

His second, fateful encounter with outsiders was in 1875, when he was 32, with the crew of the pearl fishing boat *John Bell*. When a group of sailors went ashore near Wanthaala land to get water, they reported seeing a white man among the locals they met. The captain sent them back out with tobacco and other objects, with the goal of luring Anco on board the ship under the pretext of trade. The shore crew were all Polynesian; the last and perhaps only other time Anco would have encountered people who looked like them was when he was attacked after his shipwreck. He was terrified of them. But Maademan insisted that he go try to do business, coaching him to jump overboard and swim ashore if he was detained.

But as soon as Anco stepped on board the small boat, his fears came true; he found himself staring down the barrel of a revolver. To the sailors' minds, they were rescuing him, and their guns were meant to protect him. They made a big show of firing them towards the shore, and Anco was convinced they were shooting at his family. He could understand no English, and when they brusquely gestured to him to sit still, he complied, petrified. Once on board the ship, he must have tried to jump overboard as Maademan had told him to, because he was quickly chained up for the journey.

His surroundings on the boat and in town, once familiar, were now new and overwhelming, with every sight, sound, and interaction jarring him. The clothes chafed, the food was indigestible, and the people he met were prying and condescending. But at the same time as it was strange, the familiarity of it brought back his worst memories: the shipwreck, attacks, and abandonment that had upended his childhood. He missed his Australian home and his Wanthaala family terribly.

He was taken to the nearest settler city, Somerset. A magazine writer reported that, when he arrived, he was still tied up and once on land made several escape attempts. The author added, "For some days after his arrival he sat the greater part of the day perched on the rail fence of a paddock 'like a bird,' as an eye-witness describes it, casting quick, eager, suspicious glances around him on every side and at every object that came within his view, rarely speaking, and apparently unable to remember more than a few words of his own language."

He was soon put on a steamship back to Europe. His days continued to be difficult. He never seemed comfortable in the clothes they made him wear, after not wearing any for so long. His fellow passengers reported that he was moody. Clearly he was depressed and overwhelmed. He was accustomed to sitting by squatting, about which another passenger remarked, "His habits of crouching about here and there are still those of a savage." He relied heavily on imitating what others were doing—his shipmates found this childish, but he was clearly trying to reacclimate himself to long-forgotten ways of existing in the world.

At first, he could remember no French, but it came back to him quickly, and soon he was able to tell the captain his French name, his French family members' names, his home village in France, and the story of the shipwreck. He offered very little information about his adopted family and their ways, despite everyone peppering him with questions. It's unclear if he wanted to protect them or it was simply too hard to talk about those he had just lost, much less in a foreign language.

He wrote letters to his parents, each showing his increasing capability for written French; each also contained exclamations about the most difficult parts of his time away—the Chinese migrants being attacked and killed, being abandoned by his crew, and his infected leg injury—it was as if the act of writing and thinking in French again, and being in a European context, brought these moments back to him vividly. And he still felt burning anger at the captain who had abandoned him nearly two decades before—he pledged to kill him if he ever saw him again.

As the steamship took him further away, he became resigned to his abduction. He made a plan to have his elongated right earlobe cut off, despite his pride in its length. He found that he longed to see his family of origin again; for 17 years, he'd told himself they were all dead. For his parents' part, when they received his first letter, they assumed it was a hoax until the newspaper came out the next day announcing his discovery. They had been told that he had been left for dead on a remote island and eaten by locals. They'd held his funeral, and had mourned him since.

He arrived in Saint-Gilles on January 2, the day after his 32nd birthday. One of his brothers met him at the boat, and the whole town came out to celebrate. This new stage of his adjustment was the hardest of all. Up until this point, he had been among strangers, and treated with hospitality, as a novelty and celebrity. But now he was among people who knew him, but had learned to live without him. They saw his experiences in Australia as shameful and expected him to eventually go back to being a good French person, the same person they had known many years ago.

But after the joy and novelty of his homecoming faded, he didn't get along with his family. He tried to work, but was considered too difficult. Because of his exposure to another religion, the village priest subjected him to an exorcism to cast it out. He no longer had anything in common with the community he had spent the first 13 years of his life in beyond a language and distant memories. His habits, beliefs, thoughts, tastes, and values had all shifted into something that they could not comprehend, and despite their curiosity, nobody was prepared to actually relate to him or hear about his experiences with an open mind.

All his French contemporaries knew of the place he had spent 17 years were cartoonish, racist stereotypes in which cannibalism figured heavily, and they expected him to play into those. They gave him the nickname "the Savage," which he detested. He grew more and more gruff and moody, mostly refusing to talk about his years away.

How to make a living was a problem. A local surgeon earned his trust enough to interview him for a biography telling the story of his shipwreck and time away, and this earned him some money and allowed him an outlet to tell his story more or less on his own terms, though his biographer added a good deal of embellishment and assumption. He was offered a place in a traveling show, but he turned it down after he discovered he would be billed as "the huge Anglo-Australian Giant."

He took on solitary work instead, as a lighthouse keeper. He must have found some peace, at least, in the silence and isolation. At 36, he married a 22 year old seamstress. They had no children, and he died at 50 after a career that allowed him to spend his days staring out to sea.

He never saw his Wanthaala family again. But he might have liked to know about the Australian legend that at age 37 he had sailed again for Australia and returned to the Wanthaala. For decades after his death, stories cropped up of a white-skinned, white-bearded, French-speaking man living among the Pama Malngkana of Cape York.

Barbara Thompson / Giom

Another well-documented teen castaway who integrated into an Indigenous Australian family was Barbara Crawford Thompson, who lived from 1844 to 1849 with a Kaurareg community on Ngurupai, or Horn Island, part of the Torres Strait Islands off the northern tip of Cape York, just a couple hundred miles from where Narcisse Pelletier found himself 15 years later. We don't know as much about her story as we do about Anco's, but it helps to put it in perspective with the prevailing cultures she moved between.

Europeans had been traveling to Australia since the early 1600s, and settling there since the late 1700s. Up through the late 1800s, when white Australians pretty much finished their conquest of the continent, there were a number of people with stories similar to Anco's, of being shipwrecked (or escaping from a penal colony) and being adopted by an Indigenous community. John Maynard, co-author of the book and podcast *Living with the Locals*, said, "These people weren't captives. They were refugees, and Aboriginal people took them in, fed them, and adopted them into their kinship structures and communities. There was opportunity for a genuine cultural exchange."

A central and longstanding part of many Indigenous cultures in Australian and the Torres Strait Islands is the understanding that the spirits of the dead are around us every day. Sometimes our dead loved ones return to us in living form, and when they do their skin is ghostly white. As a result of this chance of history and culture, many light-skinned Europeans who found themselves meeting Indigenous Australians in these early days experienced far warmer receptions than they expected or understood—typically far more than they offered in return. Though they did not always realize it, they were adopted back into families who were overjoyed to see their lost loved ones return to them. Even if someone was not believed to be a resurrected family member, there was no role for strangers in this time and place; adoption was the only way to bring someone into the group, even a temporary visitor.

But the white settlers' public and media at this time didn't see Aboriginal people as fully human, and they considered these adopted Europeans to be captives, held brutally against their will in inhumane conditions. If the white person in question was a woman, local settler communities would panic. Even the vaguest rumor that a white woman had been "captured" was enough for local Europeans to decide to massacre an entire Indigenous community.

In that context, we meet Barbara Crawford Thompson, whose family migrated from Scotland to Sydney, Australia when she was six years old. When she was just 12 or 13, she ran away from home and eloped with William Thompson; at that time and place, 12 was the legal minimum age for marriage. They sailed north in a small cutter with a shipwreck survivor who had invited them to join him in salvaging the wreck. But during a storm, their ship crashed into a reef and broke apart. Barbara was the only survivor. She was clinging to the wreckage when some people spotted her from land and shouted, "tuma tuma!" or *hold on* as they jumped in a canoe to come to her rescue.

As she came to shore, an old man ran out repeatedly crying out a word that she would later learn meant "daughter!" Everyone present agreed that she was his dead daughter returned to life, even bearing a resemblance in the chin and eyes. The old man was a prominent local leader named Pequi. He and his oldest wife immediately adopted her, and she was given turtle broth, water, and a place to rest and recover from the shock and injury of the wreck. They named her Giom after the daughter they had lost.

Giom was estranged from her family of origin, and presumed dead. Nobody was coming to look for her, and her energetic and independent nature helped her quickly fit into this new social world. She told a story that illustrates both her own spirit and the patience and kindness with which she was accepted. Women made ground ovens for cooking yams, and were supposed to share them with each other. Giom didn't share her oven with another woman, who threw a shell at her. Giom more than held her own: She filled the same shell with water and threw it back, and then grabbed the older woman by the hair and punched her. A crowd of onlookers cheered her on, taking her side because she was both a stranger and Pequi's daughter. But after that, the other woman became her friend and taught her to dig up yams.

In the five years that she lived with the Kaurareg, Giom sometimes saw ships stop nearby. The first time, she agonized over whether or not to try to make contact. By the time she decided that she wanted to try, it was too late. The second time, a survey ship stopped nearby, but she had a fever and was too sick to reach out. The next year that same ship returned, and her brother, knowing that she longed to reconnect, brought her to Cape York.

Giom was so tanned that the survey crew at first didn't realize she was white. When they did, they were mortified by her nudity and quickly found men's clothes for her to put on. She found a kind reception with the survey crew, and stayed on the ship, sewing a dress for herself out of their spare handkerchiefs, telling her story to the expedition's artist, who spoke some of her new language as well as English, while he took extensive notes. Her Kaurareg family members came and sat talking with her for hours at a time; the artist was struck by how kind and comfortable they all were together.

Her family were saying goodbye, and also trying to talk her out of leaving; they were heartbroken and horrified that she wanted to go. They found white people to be strange and pathetic, believing that they lived on their ships and had no country of their own, just roamed the seas eating taboo foods. What kind of future could she have with them?

She was well-loved and deeply cared for in her new home, and it's clear from her story that she had no such close family life to return to. But she decided to leave with the ship after their six weeks of work were done. "I am a Christian," was the only reason she gave, a statement perhaps of cultural as much as religious identity.

But after this, she disappears from history. The white men who were adopted into Indigenous families and returned were objects of fascination like Narcisse Pelletier; if they stayed in Australia, they were often able to work as guides and translators, keeping a foot in each culture. But that option wasn't open to a woman, much less one who was still a teenager; and in any event, widespread knowledge of her time with the Kaurareg would have doomed them.

But a generation later, they were doomed anyway. A ship was attacked near their territory in 1869 and its crew killed. Colonial authorities massacred the Kaurareg in retaliation, their genocidal rage fueled by the false rumor that they were holding the murdered captain's wife hostage (the woman turned out to be in Melbourne the entire time). The three perpetrators were later caught; they were from another island entirely.

But it was too late for the Kaurareg. Only 100 of them remained, probably less than a tenth of the population. They were moved from island to island during the early 20th century, sometimes at gunpoint, and lost a third of their remaining people to the influenza epidemic. But by the end of the century, they managed to regroup, move back to Horn Island, and resist further displacement. In 2001, a federal judge returned seven islands to Kaurareg control. In 2002, the Kaurareg declared independence from Australia, naming their new nation The United Isles of Kaiwalagal. They are still awaiting international recognition.

The Tongan Castaways

A century and a half later, in an age of GPS and satellite phones, the ocean is still a place where storms and calms can come unexpectedly, and where someone can get well and truly lost. But even those technologies weren't yet available to six Tongan teenagers who were shipwrecked on the otherwise uninhabited island of 'Ata for 15 months in the 1960s.

The boys, Sione, Stephen, Kolo, David, Luke, and Mano, were all between the ages of 13 and 15 and were students at St. Andrews, a strict, Catholic boarding school in Tongatapu, the capital of Tonga. Bored and restless, they decided to run away. They did not seem to have a unified plan; they wanted to go fishing to get a break from the terrible school food, and some of them talked about sailing on to start a new life in Fiji or even as far away as New Zealand.

They hastily packed some food and a gas burner and stole a boat from a local fisherman they disliked. They had no compass or map, and only the youngest, David, had strong sailing skills.

Their first taste of freedom was sweet. They set out on a clear day into a mellow ocean, dropping anchor five miles north of town, and fished happily for hours. When night fell, instead of setting watch, they all fell asleep. A few hours later, they woke up in the midst of a raging storm. Their sail and rudder broke, and they were adrift.

They drifted for days. They ate the food they'd brought with them and the fish they'd caught that first night. They saved the coconut shells from their dinner, and used them to catch a little water when it rained. This was all they had to drink and they shared it, each taking a sip every morning and night.

On the eighth night, they saw land—a volcanic rock jutting out of the ocean, cliffs on all sides. It was a small, uninhabited island called 'Ata, but the boys had no idea where they were, or even what direction they had sailed in. Rigging the boat's blanket as a sail, they made for land. Mano volunteered to go ashore first. He was so weak from hunger and dehydration that he could barely swim to shore, and when he got there he crawled to the grass and fell down; he couldn't stand up. He could only summon the strength to call back to the other boys that he had made it.

As they tried to steer the boat in, it broke apart on the rocks, and they came to shore covered in cuts and bruises, without a means of leaving again. Mano told *The Guardian* many years later, "We were very happy, but the first thing we did, we say a prayer, thank God for what he brought us to." Desperately thirsty, they killed some sea birds, drank their blood, and ate their eggs raw. "After that," Mano remembered, "we all fell down there and sleep until the sunrise the next morning woke us up."

That first day, they acted quickly to figure out what they needed to survive. Sione described the process later to a documentary film crew. "First, a fire. We had no matches, but we hungered for warm food. Stephen remembered the old ways of making a flame. It took many hours, but eventually we did have a fire, and from this day onward it was never left unattended."

Next, water. Sione recalled, "From my father's teaching, I remembered a way to obtain water. There are trees on the island that have water in their trunks. With wooden stakes and rough knives, it takes four days to dig deep. But then, drip by drip, we have water."

Food was problematic at first, but being able to cook helped immensely. They ate more of the wild birds that nested on the island, plus eggs, green bananas, wild greens, fish, tortoise, and coconuts. As they explored the mountain, their possibilities opened up. Halfway up the cliff, they found some very old knives. This was a real breakthrough, Sione said: "We cut the tops off young coconuts and drank the juice. For the first time since we landed here three months before, we were happy. We had the will and the strength to go on."

At the top of the mountain, they found the remains of a settlement, uninhabited for nearly a century.[1] Beans and other crops were growing wild,

1 This was 'Ata's lone village, Kotomaile, where 350 people lived in the mid-19th Century. In 1863, 144 people—nearly half the population—were invited onto a ship, the *Grecian*, ostensibly to trade. Instead, the hatches were sealed behind them and they were kidnapped into slavery (by one account, the town's mayor colluded with the slavers; his descendants remain besmirched by this rumor to this day). The ship's captain was Thomas McGrath, an Australian

and feral chickens ran the place. Every night they chased down chickens for dinner, turning it into a game, but eventually built traps and domesticated them, feeding them coconuts and scraps from their meals, breeding them, and feasting on their eggs. They only ate the chickens when it was too stormy to catch the wild birds.

The two oldest boys took responsibility for the group. Stephen, with his practical skills, took charge of their material survival, and Sione, a natural leader, managed conflict resolution and led them in daily prayers and hymns. They made a house on the site of the old settlement, cutting palm fronds for the roof, which helped them protect their fire from the rain. They used the knives to carve tree trunks into buckets for storing rainwater. They settled into a routine, and soon it was expanded beyond mere survival. They set up a tennis court, a boxing ring, and a gym with hand weights, and exercised every day. "We knew that if we became lazy, nature would beat us," said Sione. Kolo made a ukulele out of the materials at hand, and they sang and composed songs together.

They worked in teams of two, in regular shifts. Two boys climbed onto the cliffs every day, aiming to catch two wild birds for each boy. One day, Mano and Stephen were out hunting and, as Sione recalled it, "Stephen decided to go further down the cliff face, where there were more nests. Then he slipped and fell. We found him on a narrow ledge 40 feet below. His leg was broken." They treated the injury with hot coconut fronds, the way they had learned growing up. They knew what they were doing—Stephen's leg healed well and in four months, he could walk again.

---

who'd been deported to Tasmania at 16. He had the ship on a whaling commission but found the kidnapping business, known as "blackbirding," to be more profitable. In just 2 years, 3,000 Pacific Islanders were abducted in this way and brought to Peru as part of that country's campaign to "recruit" laborers to mine guano—layers of bird droppings built up over centuries on islands—at that time a major global commodity, used as fertilizer.

But the 'Atans never made it to Peru; the government had canceled all labor contracts due to international scandal about the use of slave labor. The Peruvian government paid another captain, also a slaver, to return the 'Atans and 300 other kidnapped Pacific Islanders home; instead he took the money and marooned them on a desert island. There was a smallpox outbreak, and by the time a whaler found them three weeks later, only half were still alive. By the time a Peruvian warship could be sent to pick them up, only 38 people had survived. They were brought to the town of Paita in Peru, where most stayed.

The 200 'Atans who had not been kidnapped were relocated by Tongan King George Tupou I to the island of 'Eua, for protection from future raids. After his contract ran out, Captain McGrath failed to return the *Grecian* to her owner and was arrested shortly after for tax evasion, but he was never brought to justice for his acts on 'Ata.

The boys were healthy, well-fed, resilient, resourceful, and worked well together as a team. But their time on the island was also a scary and lonely experience. "We were often unhappy, and at times we argued," Sione said. "And then we would walk away from our friends into the jungle. Sometimes we would cry a little." Sione and Stephen in particular would have disagreements about leadership, and one of them would need to cool off after these conflicts by hiking across the island and camping alone for a few days.

Rescue and escape were never far from their minds. They tried to build a raft, but it wrecked a mile off shore and they had to swim back to the island—just as well, as they'd set off towards the open ocean. As months went by, they gave up hope of escaping. "At times, it seemed like we had been on 'Ata forever," Sione said. But they still kept a constant lookout at the highest cliff. Ships passed within sight of their lookout four times. They were ready for this and lit large signal fires, but none of them stopped.

And then came the fifth boat. The captain was Peter Warner, who had been a teen runaway himself. His father, a radio and electronics tycoon, had been the richest man in Australia. Peter chafed at the prospect of joining the family business, and ran away to sail around the world working on ships, eventually becoming a captain. By 1966, he had returned home and joined the family business as an accountant, but ran a side business with his fishing fleet. On one trip, he took a detour to look for new crayfish grounds in sight of 'Ata, and noticed burn marks on the cliff faces. This seemed strange—natural wildfires aren't common in the humid tropics—so he steered his ship closer to look. His crew heard voices first, then saw wild, naked boys with long hair waving their arms and shouting. Stephen leaped into the water and swam out to the boat, followed by the others.

Captain Warner and his all-white crew were alarmed to see unkempt brown men swimming quickly towards them. Assuming they were criminals, they loaded their rifles and prepared to repel the boarders. But then Stephen reached the boat and his huge, delighted smile set the captain at ease. He lowered the ladder, and was further impressed by Stephen's announcement, in boarding school English, that there were six castaways and that they had been on the island for about 15 months (their timekeeping was off by only 2 days).

"Good story," thought the captain, "but I don't believe it." The boys were surely too healthy and strong to be desperate castaways. Warner let the boys all board the boat and showed them photographs, testing their story, asking them about Tongan life and politics. Their answers broke down his skepticism more. He asked for their names and got on the radio and called the operator to investigate, who put him on hold for 20 minutes, during which time the boys wolfed down and then vomited up their first western food in more than a year. The operator came back on the air in tears, saying, "It's a miracle!" The boys had been presumed dead—their families had searched for them for months, and eventually held funerals for them.

Warner and his crew unloaded their guns, gave the boys their spare clothes, and found them places to sleep. The next day, the boys gave the crew a tour of the island. Then the ship turned back the way it had just come and brought them home to Tonga.

Returning home was joyous and also nerve-wracking. Sione recalls thinking, "We hope our families don't think we have changed too much. A few of us had girlfriends, too. Perhaps they won't remember." Warner had sent a message to a media contact in Sydney, so when they arrived back home, camera crews were waiting to capture the homecoming. So was almost the entire population of their island, nearly 900 people.

They were greeted with tears and 3 days of feasting. One night, Captain Warner threw a party on his boat in their honor, but they didn't show up. He went to look for them and couldn't find them anywhere. Finally around 1am, he discovered that they were in jail—the owner of the boat they'd stolen had decided to press charges and had them arrested. Warner used his family connections to sell the Australian film rights to their story, and used that money to buy a replacement for the stolen boat. Later that year, they all returned to the island to re-enact their survival on camera for a documentary crew.

The King of Tonga offered Captain Warner a reward; he asked for, and received, fishing rights in the kingdom. He built a new ship for the purpose, named the *Ata,* and hired all six returned castaways on as part of his crew.

The boys all grew up to lead different lives, but the skills and resilience learned on 'Ata stayed with each of them.

Tevita Fatai "Stephen" Latu, whose ingenuity ensured the group always had fire, water, and food, became an engineer, and has passed away.

Luke Veikoso kept up his practice from the island and became a professional boxer. He was the South Seas heavyweight champion in 1976. After retiring, he emigrated to the US, initially moving in with Sione in Oakland, California. The two remain good friends.

Sione 'Ulufonua Fataua, the group's spiritual leader, is now the head pastor for the Church of Tonga's 16 congregations in the US. He has lived in Oakland, Portland, and now Salt Lake City.

Kolo Fekitoa, who built the ukelele, stayed in Tonga and worked as a fisherman. In 2015, told he only had a few years to live, he returned to 'Ata with a documentary film crew to live for 10 days in the same way he had as a teen. It was his last wish. He passed away in 2017.

Sione "Mano" Totau lives in Australia, just down the road from Peter Warner, and the two remain close friends and business partners. In 1974, when Mano was a crewmember of the *Ata*, they were weathering a gale when they came upon a Japanese longliner that had run aground on a rocky reef. Its crew of four had been stuck there for six weeks, living on fish and canned food. At the time Mano and Peter rescued them, the four hated each others' guts, and were down to their last pack of matches. After years of working on Peter's ships, Mano became a captain in his own right.

Tevita "David" Siola'a lives in Auckland, New Zealand. In 2020, an article about their experience went viral and the story rights were optioned for a Hollywood movie. David and the other three living castaways are consultants on the film.

Conclusion, sources, and further reading

To have survived a great trauma, to be separated from your home and community, to have been close to death and done difficult, dangerous, uncomfortable, and downright gross things—these experiences leave a huge impression on your entire life. And everyone handles it differently, depending on what they brought going into it.

We can't know, but Manjirō's seemingly natural ability to make lasting friendships wherever he went, to endlessly adapt to different cultures, and even his class mobility, all point towards a healthy, supportive, loving family upbringing. It seems likely that he learned a strong sense of self and social skills from an early age. That doesn't mean he was naturally a better person or more likely to be successful or liked—simply that the disruption of his childhood was a singular event rather than a constant one, and therefore perhaps more easily recovered from.

On the other end of the spectrum, Narcisse Pelletier suffered a series of disruptions from at least age 12, and was already in an unstable environment when he was shipwrecked; the subsequent attack, long voyage, and abandonments compounded that. His depression and utter loneliness after his return to France suggests that he may not have been entirely unlonely there the first time around, either. And in a very different vein, Barbara Thompson's method of dealing with conflict was to go all in, fists flying, an aggressive tactic she surely learned early in life, and which, in the friendly new environment she found herself in after her shipwreck, could be compensated for and neutralized with love.

Perhaps the most successful survivors were the six Tongan castaways in the final chapter; they did find themselves alone on an island. Their existing friendship, the skills and habits they'd learned from their supportive families, and perhaps also the shared expectations they brought from the regimented boarding school environment they were running away from, their quick return to a supportive environment, and their ability to stay close with each other all seem to have softened the impact of their situation.

It's hard to know what all of the people in these stories were thinking and feeling, beyond what they (or their biographers) chose to share afterwards. But reading between the lines, there's a lot to relate with. And it's hard not to see these stories, and wonder how we would behave in similar situations, what decisions we would make, where we would thrive and where we would break, who would be our friends, and whether or not we'd want to return to where we came from.

In researching this zine, I tried to use primary sources as much as they were available in English. They're all compelling to read, and not too difficult to find, if you want to dive deeper.

To read more about Manjirō:
When he returned to Japan, Manjirō spent a year giving an incredibly detailed account of his ten years away to his interrogators—not just what he did and who he met, but the customs, fashions, cultures, and politics he observed along the way. This must have come across as speculative fiction to the officials who had never left the island. After he, Denzo, and Goemon were returned to his home province, 27 year old Kawada Shoryo, a scholar and artist, was brought in to translate and illustrate their story. He and Manjirō became close friends, exchanging knowledge and language skills. The result was a beautiful, 4-volume book, titled *Hyoson Kirykau,* which translates to *A Brief Account of Drifting Toward the Southeast*. It was written in calligraphy with watercolor illustrations that are fascinating, showing scenes of New England life rendered by an artist only familiar with Japanese architecture and fashion. The book was completed less than a year before the Black Ships came with their guns to force their peace treaty, and as a result, it suddenly became sought-after reading for officials who wanted to understand these US Americans. Supposedly it inspired one of the great modernizers of Japan, Sakamoto Ryoma, by introducing him to the idea of democracy. Since the copies had to be made by hand, few were ever created and it was largely forgotten in the decades that followed. A museum curator found one at a book fair in 1912, bringing it back to scholarly attention, but it wasn't mass-produced until the 1960s.

Manjirō was telling his story in part to satisfy his government's need for information about the rest of the world, but he was also on trial; the most obvious way this affected his story is that he was careful to avoid an entire topic that would have been fundamental to his life in New England. Admitting to Christian beliefs, or even to having been exposed to them, could have resulted in his execution. Similarly to Anco, despite the intense religiousness of the culture he'd been immersed in during his time away, in his account it simply doesn't exist.

There is a recent translation of the book with a lot of interesting commentary, context, and fact-checking. It seems to be out of print except in ebook:

Kawada, Ikaku (ed)., Nakahama, Manjirō, Kikuoka, Michael T. *Drifting Toward the Southeast: The Story of Five Japanese Castaways*. Spinner Publications, 2003.

To read more about Otokichi:

You're on your own here, I'm afraid. There's not a lot of information about Otokichi to be found online, and much of it is contradictory and badly sourced. I included the story anyway without having found a primary source in English, and apologize for the misinformation that's likely found its way into the story as a result.

To read more about Anco:

Just a few years after returning to France, Anco dictated his story to a surgeon and all around scholar named Constant Merland, who offered to help him write it down so he could answer people's burning questions and also make some money. Merland, writing his story, recounts in vivid detail Anco's adventures up until the time he first was taken to the Wanthaala community. Then he stops the narrative and launches into a detailed, if condescending and partly made-up, ethnography. This section seems to be deeply colored by Merland's assumptions, as he filled in the gaps where Anco declined to share. For instance, the religious beliefs Anco would have been initiated into were a secret to be shared only with other initiates; Merland took his silence on spiritual questions to mean that the Wanthaala had no spiritual beliefs at all. And Merland's account is full of racist, colonialist assumptions about property rights, hygiene, beauty, and even the idea baked into the organization of the book that Indigenous people (or as he calls them throughout, "savages") somehow live in an unchanging way, with no sense of history.

The English translation of Merland's book is reprinted in Stephanie Anderson's scholarly book *Pelletier*, along with extensive context and commentary based on other firsthand accounts of people who met Pelletier before and after his time with the Wanthaala. His time in Australia is put in context of the work of modern anthropologists and linguists, and I've used Anderson's suggested spellings here (e.g., Anco instead of the "Amglo" transcribed by Merland).

Anderson, Stephanie. *Pelletier: The Forgotten Castaway of Cape York*. Australia: Melbourne Books, 2012.

I'm also indebted to John Maynard and Victoria Haskins' *Living with the Locals*, which sensitively recounts the stories Narcisse Pelletier, Barbara Thompson, and more white settlers who lived with indigenous groups in what are now Australia and the Torres Islands, with a particular empathy for Aboriginal perspectives on these events. It's a difficult-to-find academic book, but they've recorded several podcasts which cast these stories in a very poignant and relatable light.

Maynard, John and Haskins, Victoria. *Living with the Locals: Early Europeans' Experience of Indigenous Life*. National Library of Australia, 2016.

Also check out the *Living with the Locals* authors on this podcast episode on Anco: *www.abc.net.au/radio/programs/speakingout/lwtl-pelletier/9759738*

And another on Giom: *www.abc.net.au/radio/programs/speakingout/barbara-thompson/9710230*

To learn more about the Tongan castaways

Everyone on Tonga knows the story of the six castaway teens, but it came to the world's attention in early 2020, after an article about them was published by Dutch author Rutger Bregman in *The Guardian*, an excerpt from his book *Humankind*. The article fascinated the world and was shared over 7 million times, and a Hollywood production company bought the rights to make a feature film. It also garnered controversy—and fairly so. For starters, Bregman centered the story around Captain Warner's experiences and perspective, without any acknowledgment of the region's colonial and racist history that played out even in this ultimately happy story; for instance, Bregman doesn't share that Warner initially had his crew point guns at the castaways. Perhaps stranger, the author bent the story to fit his book's thesis that humans have a universally altruistic nature, comparing it with the dystopian novel *Lord of the Flies* about a group of schoolboys stranded on an island who destroy each other. He used this story to "prove" that when left to our own devices humans will work together harmoniously rather than destroy each other. But he seems to have failed to take into account cultural and class differences; unlike the cutthroat upper class British boarding school culture which was fictionalized and drawn out to its most extreme conclusion in *Lord of the Flies*, Tongan culture prizes cooperation, and the boys came from poor families where sharing resources was necessary for survival and where they had learned the practical and social skills they needed to feed, house, and organize themselves.

As this zine goes to print, the story of the Tongan castaways is still unfolding on the internet, and that is the best place to learn more. By searching for their names, you can find contemporary interviews with many of the men, articles and documentary footage from the 1960s, and commentary about their experience and about the way it is being told, by whom, and to whom.

The original, ten-minute-long documentary that bailed them out of jail, narrated by Sione, is on YouTube: *http://microcosm.pub/castawaysdoc*

The tragic story of 'Ata's previous residents is told in the book:

Hamilton, Scott. *The Stolen Island: Searching for 'Ata*. Bridget William Books (New Zealand), 2016.